♥ Mrs. Grossman's
HOLIDAY STICKER IDEA BOOK™

Celebrate all year long with spectacular sticker crafts!

Mrs. Grossman wishes to thank the following artists who
have contributed original designs to this book:
Linda Risbrudt, Linda Hendrickson, Audrey Giorgi,
Julie Cohen, Melissa Carlson, Susan Pratt, Gigi Sproul,
Sue Ferguson and Susanna Gallisdorfer.

Written by Mary Clasen.
Designed by Susan Pratt, Melissa Carlson,
Julie Cohen, Gigi Sproul and Andrea Grossman
with help from Blythe Omick and Raul Chacon.
Photography by Waldo Bascom.
Styling by Angie Heinrich and Audrey Giorgi.

Many thanks to the following people who have offered
ideas, counsel and encouragement:
Calvin Goodman, Patti Johnson, Bonnie Loizos,
Dee and Warren Gruenig.

©1997 Mrs. Grossman's Paper Company
All rights reserved. The material in this book is intended
for personal use only. It may not be photocopied,
nor may the designs be employed in any products
used for commercial use without written
permission from Mrs. Grossman's Paper Company, Inc.

Mrs. Grossman's™ and Mrs. Grossman's Paper Company™
are trademarks of Mrs. Grossman's Paper Company, Inc.

Printed in the United States of America

Mrs. Grossman's Paper Company
Mrs. Grossman's Holiday Idea Book
ISBN: 0-910299021

Published by Mrs. Grossman's Paper Company
3810 Cypress Drive, Petaluma, California 94954
Distributed in Canada by Pierre Belvédère
Distributed in Japan by Sony Plaza Company, Ltd.

TABLE OF CONTENTS

All About Stickers..4

Tools..6

Storage..7

Techniques..8

Design Basics..12

Beyond the Basics..14

Ready, Set, Sticker!..15

One Minute Magic 16

Valentine's Day..18

Easter..22

Summer Holidays..26

Halloween...30

Thanksgiving...34

Christmas..38

Resources..44

Meet the Artists...45

Sticker Checklist..46

ALL ABOUT STICKERS

Here are some general terms, definitions and hints to make sticker art even more creative and fun. We also address some common questions: What is a sticker module? How do I find the stickers I want? Where should—and shouldn't—I put stickers? The answers are right here!

Regular **R**

Double Regular **DR**

Giant **G**

Extravagant **E**

Modules

MODULE
Our entire line is based on a modular system. Module is the term for the sticker or stickers between perforation marks. Some modules contain one sticker, while others contain an entire collection!

SIZE
Stickers come in sizes from micro flowers to extravagant rabbits. Some stickers, like the bear, are available in three sizes, but most are designed in the scale we found works best with other stickers.

LINER PAPER
This is the waxy paper stickers are on when you buy them. Save those liner papers! Later, you'll learn how to use them to build perfect sticker compositions.

BACK PRINTING
This is the information on back of the liner paper. Turn any Mrs. Grossman's sticker over and discover some great sticker ideas! You'll also find the name of the designer, a size and price code and the year the sticker was created and copyrighted.

Back printing

DAMS
These are small, extra pieces found inside sticker designs. Remove the dams before you put the sticker down. If you miss one, you get to say "dam!" and remove it with an X-ACTO knife.

MIRROR IMAGE
This refers to identical sticker shapes printed facing opposite directions. This allows you to maximize flexibility in your sticker art, and place stickers back-to-back for 3-D designs.

MATERIAL
This is the type of paper used to make a sticker. Most of our stickers are printed on shiny, high-gloss paper. Some are printed with special film, materials and techniques.

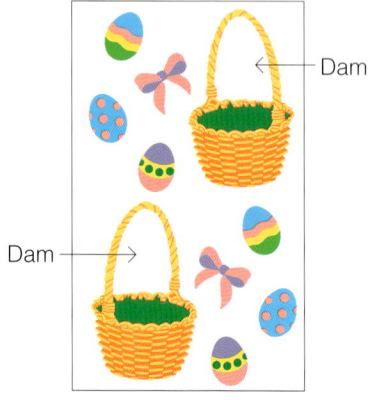
Dams

Mirror Image

4

Stickers are like smiles. They get your thoughts across without words.

HOW DO I AVOID TEARING STICKERS?
When removing stickers, start at the bottom and lift upwards, slowly peeling the sticker off the liner paper. If a sticker is difficult to remove, try bending the liner paper back first. With long or skinny stickers, lift part of the image, bend the liner paper back, press the exposed section in place, then peel up the rest of the liner paper.

WHERE CAN I PUT STICKERS?
Stickers really love paper! Cards, envelopes, gift bags, gift wrap, lunch bags, stationery—you name it! They can be used on other surfaces, too. However, we do not recommend placing stickers on furniture, painted walls, silk, leather, suede or vinyl.

OOPS! HOW DO I REMOVE STICKERS?
On wood or glass, apply some light furniture or salad oil, let it sit for a few minutes, then peel off the sticker. For other surfaces, we recommend using one of the gentle commercial solvent products available.

WHAT IS A COPYRIGHT?
Every Mrs. Grossman's sticker has been created by a trained designer, and is protected legally by a copyright. This means our stickers are meant to be used and enjoyed for personal use—but cannot be reproduced or sold on any item for commercial purposes.

HOW DO I FIND THE STICKERS I WANT?
Our stickers are sold in stationery and specialty stores, card shops, toy and craft stores and mail-order catalogs. Need help finding the stickers you want in your area? Call us at 800/429-4549 or visit our Website at www.mrsgrossmans

ARE THESE STICKERS ACID FREE?
Mrs. Grossman's frequently submits all of our materials to an independent lab for pH testing. The results verify that our stickers are virtually acid free. Our stickers should be safe for use in photo albums as long as the stickers are not placed directly on the photos. The subject of creating "archival" photo albums is a complicated one, and there are many factors to be aware of. We invite you to send for our complimentary info sheet, "Facts, Fiction and Fun: Helpful Tips on Scrapbooking."

Having the right tools at hand allows you to create effective, professional-looking sticker art with ease. We recommend the following tools:

SCISSORS A pair of good quality scissors is your most important tool, the one absolute essential. They should be sharp, maneuverable, comfortable and pointy, with long blades.

X-ACTO KNIFE Craft knives are great for lifting and placing stickers (especially tiny pieces) as well as trimming stickers and paper. You can also use this knife with a ruler to cut stickers perfectly straight. Caution! These blades are really sharp so be extra careful and always put the cover on when not in use.

TWEEZERS Pointy tweezers will help you move small pieces and reach into tight areas. They are useful for lifting stickers and placing them just where you want them.

RULER A straight edge is often helpful to measure, center a design or help establish your ground line.

POWDER What do you do when you don't want a sticker to stick? Put powder or cornstarch on the back to neutralize the adhesive.

PAINT PEN Indispensable for adding sparkle and charm to your sticker art, these pens will write on even the shiniest surfaces. We recommend silver, gold and black.

MOUNTING TAPE Give your stickers a lift! Mounting tape makes them rise off the page and gives your sticker art dimension.

GLUE STICK or DOUBLE-STICK TAPE Not everything we use is sticky! Keep this on hand to attach different colored papers or accessories to your sticker art.

MRS. GROSSMAN'S STICKER COMPANIONS Choose from a rainbow of colorful bags, bookmarks and cards designed expressly for use with our stickers. Keep a supply of colored cards, paper and envelopes on hand.

FUN EXTRAS Thread, ribbon, string, paper punches, deckle scissors and specialty papers are great accessories for your sticker art.

STICKER STORAGE

Simplify project set-up by storing stickers in a box by category. Keep stickers clean, dry and away from light, and they'll last indefinitely! To get you started, we recommend a sturdy box, separated into the following categories:

Hearts   Party   Accessories
Animals Holiday Flowers
Nature   Sports   Words and symbols

Keep an ample supply of the stickers you use frequently, and always file away a few favorites and extras of any new styles.

Any large box with a lid can hold a sticker collection, but none beats our Sticker File Box™. The dividers allow you to file by category so you can find the stickers you want when you want them. The lid keeps them dry, dust free and stays open while you work. Your tools will fit in the box, too.

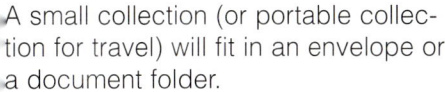

A small collection (or portable collection for travel) will fit in an envelope or a document folder.

A three-ring binder is another good storage method. Use archival pocket pages in the binder to avoid damaging the stickers.

Techniques

This section is filled with tricks-of-the-trade and practice projects. We've chosen some fun designs to illustrate the basic techniques.

CUTTING
Cutting is a basic sticker art technique. You can use scissors or an X-ACTO knife. Some of us prefer one tool for everything, while others vary the tool as needed.

The rabbit used in this project extends past the boundaries of the card. Put it on the card, still on the liner paper, so you can decide where to place it. You will be able to see the border of the card through the sticker. Mark the cutting line with a ruler and pencil.

CUTTING WITH SCISSORS
Keep the line clean and straight as you cut this large sticker. Always leave your stickers on the liner paper when you cut them to keep your scissors clean.

CUTTING WITH A KNIFE
An X-ACTO knife makes a very clean cut, and is especially handy for avoiding choppy edges on larger stickers. Put the sticker on the card and place the ruler along the border. Draw the edge of the knife along the ruler and remove leftover pieces.

LIFTING
Pull stickers off the liner paper slowly to avoid tearing them. Watch out for those rabbit ears!

POWDERING
When you don't want a sticker—or part of a sticker—to stick, use powder or cornstarch to neutralize the adhesive. Pat it gently on the back of the sticker and wipe off the excess from the sticker and card. We use it here behind the rabbit's ear to make it look floppy.

Cutting with scissors

Cutting with a knife

Lifting

Powdering

When it comes to stickers, little touches make a big impression!

BACK-TO-BACK
These balloons not only rise above the picture, but look good on both sides. Almost all of Mrs. Grossman's stickers are printed in mirror image to make it easy to achieve this effect.

Place the first balloon so that it extends above the card. Open the card and put another balloon behind the first one, lining up the edges and sticking the bottom of the balloon to inside of the card. The second balloon can be a different color.

EMBELLISHMENTS
The balloon string here is drawn freehand with a paint pen or permanent marker. If you prefer, use a ruler to make the strings appear taut.

For a more dimensional look, use real string or ribbon for the balloon strings. Use your knife to cut around his paw, lift the paw up and slip the ribbon or string underneath. Tuck the other end under the bottom of the balloons.

3-D EFFECTS
Stickers that pop off the page add even more dimension to your work. Use a small piece of mounting tape on the back of the sticker, leaving the protective backing on the tape. Powder the back of the sticker, but not the tape. Remove the backing from the tape and press the sticker to the card.

FINAL
Congratulations! You've made a delightful Easter card!

Back to back

Using a pen

Using a paint pen

3-dimensional

Finished card

Joyful holiday messages are as easy as pumpkin pie! Here are a few basic holiday designs that catch the eye. For more of these easy-and-fun activities, look for Mrs. Grossman's Basic Sticker Idea Book, too!

Another essential skill for sticker art is deciding which sticker to apply first. These simple, step-by-step designs will help you practice that skill. If you need to lift a sticker—or part of a sticker—that's already in place, use your X-ACTO knife or a corner of the liner paper. Then you'll be able to slip the next sticker underneath.

This section also helps you remember to group stickers. Keep the action together! As you copy these designs, think about how you would change them to make them your own.

Near each design you'll find the names of the stickers used. Sometimes we only use one or two stickers from a module. Save those extra stickers. Refer to the sticker list in the back of the book to identify the modules.

BUILDING WITH STICKERS

Here's an easy trick to help you build perfect sticker combinations before they even touch down! Choose stickers that will convey your message, provide a focal point or main character and supply a fun setting. Ready? Now try these two techniques for adjusting the placement of each sticker as you build:

Fingertips

Build simple combinations on your fingertips, adjusting the stickers until the image is picture perfect, then place your design on the desired surface.

Liner Paper

Build more complex designs on left-over Extravagant module liner paper. Rebuild to your heart's content, then place the design as one sticker on your background.

Fingertips

Liner Paper

10

EASTER RABBIT
Easter Rabbit, Grass.

DRESSED-UP BEAR
Bear, Small Leaves, Giant Pumpkin Faces.

GINGERBREAD BOY
Holly, Gingerbread Boy.

11

DESIGN BASICS

PLACEMENT
It's easy to create effective designs when you learn how to combine and position stickers on a card.

By grouping sticker images you create visual order in your picture. Then the space around and between stickers (negative space) brings attention to the stickered image (focal point).

You can position your sticker images on the card in the center...

on a diagonal...

to the edge of the card...

or beyond the edge.

PLANNING
Have a plan before you start stickering. Know what you want to say and select the stickers that suit your message.

As you plan your composition, hold the stickers over the card to see exactly where you want to place them. Put them down lightly in case you want to move one or tuck one sticker behind another.

Add excitement, drama and motion to your designs. This card suggests movement and activity in a complete, colorful scene.

Mrs. Grossman's stickers are purposely made to be used together, so designing is simple, and the possibilities are limitless! Start by practicing the four basic concepts shown here: placement, planning, depth and story. Then add the most important element—your personal touch—to make the images come to life!

DEPTH
Placing stickers together in a group gives your design a sense of depth.

Stickers scattered all over the card appear to float.

A ground line (horizontal line or plane) gives your sticker image a place to rest.

Where you place the ground line will convey distance...

or closeness.

It can be a drawn line or an imaginary one.

TELL A STORY
Trick-or-treaters set off for a night of spooky fun.

Frolicking children celebrate on Easter morning.

This scene uses all of the Design Basics to tell an imaginative story filled with fun!

BEYOND THE BASICS

What's the secret to creating advanced sticker art? Just combine the techniques, design skills and special effects you've learned—all in one project! Feel free to refer back to the front sections of the book as needed, then try these fun-to-make examples:

COMPLEX SIMPLICITY
- Prominent center placement
- Intricate layered effect
- Trimmed to the edge stickers

POP-UP, OUT AND OFF
- Trimmed and decorated bags
- 3-D effects with mounting tape
- Powdered, over the edge stickers
- Thoughtful sticker grouping

TEXTURES AND BACKGROUNDS
- Simple, eye-catching design
- 3-D effects with mounting tape
- Colorful, contrasting papers
- Over the edge stickers

In the rest of this book, you'll follow colorful examples, read step-by-step instructions—and create amazing sticker art!

The sections ahead offer six exciting themes: Valentine's Day, Easter, Summer Holidays, Halloween, Thanksgiving, Christmas and Chanukah. Each section includes sticker art activities, useful tips, and an entire page of extra design ideas. Some projects have detailed instructions, while others are so straightforward, you can simply copy the picture.

YOU'RE THE ARTIST
Remember, the ideas in this book are just the beginning! There's no end to the creative projects you can make with stickers. It's okay to change and rearrange stickers to make your own brand new designs. So go ahead. Explore uncharted territories! Throw away the map!

PUTTING IT ALL TOGETHER
- Layered stickers
- Paint pen accents
- Multiple ground lines
- Trimmed, contrasting papers
- Thoughtful placement and grouping
- 3-D effects with mounting tape
- Powdered, over the edge stickers

ONE MINUTE MAGIC

Sticker art is for everybody! It's fun, quick, clean and affordable. Best of all, whether you use five or fifty stickers, your designs will always be a delight to make, give, and receive. Start with these projects that use less than five stickers to create instant messages!

FRIENDLY ADVICE
- Set up the work area so stickers and tools are handy.
- Flip back to the front sections if you need a refresher course.
- It's okay to experiment and change designs.
- It's okay to cut or use part of a sticker.
- It's okay to overlap stickers.
- It's okay to enjoy yourself!

THANKSGIVING BOOKMARK
Pilgrims, Giant Trees, Color Dots.

SPRINGTIME GIFT CARD
Reflections Watering Can, Easter Rabbit.

SUMMER BEAR GIFT CARD
Expressions Bear, Flag.

MICE-IN-LOVE MINI GIFT BAG
Red Heart, Dressed Mice.

CHRISTMAS GREETING CARD
Small Santa, Sleigh, Reindeer.

It doesn't take much to make magic with stickers.

SANTA-GATOR GIFT BAG
Extravagant Animal Expressions, Santa Hats, Candy Canes.

ROSE BOW MINI GIFT BAG
Rose, Multi Bows.

GOLFER BEAR BOOKMARK
Bear, Golf.

GHOSTLY GIFT CARD
Jack-o'-Lantern, Small Ghosts.

COZY COTTAGE GREETING CARD
Giant House, Small Flags, Ivy.

VALENTINE'S DAY

PENGUIN GIFT CARD
Penguins, Small Sparkle Hearts, Confetti.
Cut the Penguin's arm to hold a heart. A confetti square cut diagonally makes a perfect bow tie!

ROSY BOUQUET GREETING CARD
Roses, Micro Hearts, Christmas Bow.
Trim a white card and attach it with mounting tape to a red card for a dimensional look. Assemble the roses on a piece of liner paper, then place them on the card and add the bow.

LOVE LETTER GIFT TAG
Reflection Letter, Micro Hearts, Design Lines Primaries.
Add a red Design Line to a white card to make the border, then add the stickers.

RABBIT MINI BAG
Extravagant Rabbit, Small Sparkle Hearts, Top Hat.
Place the rabbit as shown, trimming off any excess sticker. Use a silver paint pen to add magical dots.

HEART GARLAND GREETING CARD
Small Roses, Giant Red Heart (optional).
For a perfect shape, trace around a giant heart sticker (still on the liner paper) with a pencil. It works just like a stencil, and you can use the sticker later! Cut the leaves and stems off of the roses. Place the flowers on the drawn line. Use the leaves to fill in the design.

Whether you want to embellish a romantic love letter, or help the kids make cards for the entire class—stickers encourage the true spirit of Valentine's Day. Speaking of kids, add a few stickers to each school Valentine for a welcome (no-sugar) surprise!

WRAPPED ROSE
Red and Pink Micro Hearts.
Wrap up the rose and tie it with a pretty ribbon. Place the hearts on the cellophane in a scattered pattern.

LEAPING HEARTS GIFT BOX
Small Sparkle Hearts, Reflections Small Hearts.
Place the hearts back-to-back on some thin wire. Secure the wire ends inside the box with tape. Use the reflections hearts on the box.

MINI ROSE GIFT TAG
Small Roses.
Trim a piece of white paper and attach it to a larger black piece. Punch a hole for the ribbon.

LOVE NOTES GREETING CARD
Sparkle Hugs and Kisses, Sparkle Multi Micro Hearts, Giant Musical Instruments, Micro Flowers.
Trim a pretty piece of specialty paper and attach it to a red card. Place the stickers to one side for a dramatic effect.

 *Making a card? Use extra stickers to decorate the envelope!*

BE MINE VALENTINES
Penguins, Giant Red Heart, Micro Hearts, Confetti Hearts, Giant Bear, Sparkle Bow, Cinnamon Hearts.
Glue a heart-shaped doily to red paper and cut around the edge of the doily. Add a few stickers that convey your heart-felt message.

GARDEN CAT GIFT BAG
Micro Hearts, Extravagant Geometrics, Giant Cats, Garden Border, Ivy.
Draw the fence on thick white paper and cut it out with an X-ACTO knife. Attach it to the bag with mounting tape. Attach the cat with mounting tape, powdering the back of the sticker, but not the mounting tape. Add the remaining stickers, powdering any that extend beyond the edge. Use a paint pen for the accents.

HIS AND HERS GIFT BAGS
Sparkle Bow, Opalescent Party Glasses, Small Roses, Multi Bows.
His: Cut a V in the front of a black mini bag and glue a white 3" x 5" card inside. Add the bow, bubble buttons and boutonniere rose.
Hers: Fold a doily in half and cut a circle out of the middle. Fit the inside circle over a red mini bag, and cut around it to make the neckline. Glue the doily in place and add the bow.

SWEETHEART GIFT BOX
Micro Hearts, Sparkle Hugs and Kisses.
Place coordinating stickers on the ribbon and gift tag for a wrap job that rivals the gift!

There are so many ways to say "I love you" with stickers.

EASTER

MINI GIFT BAG MASTERPIECE
Clouds and Rain, Garden Border, Easter Rabbit, Rainbow, Daffodils, Opalescent Sun, Moon and Stars.
Cut the top edge of a green mini bag with craft scissors to look like a hilltop. Cut the top edge of a yellow mini bag and nest it inside of the green one. Place the stickers as shown, powdering the backs of any that extend beyond the edge.

PRETTY PLACE CARDS
Easter Basket, Reflection Eggs.
Use contrasting sheets of colorful paper and attach stickers with mounting tape. Powder the back of the handle where it extends over the edge of the card.

SPRINGTIME NOTE CARD
Pink Phlox, Calla Lily.
Assemble the flowers on a piece of liner paper. Cut the bottom straight across and apply to a pretty note card. Use mounting tape behind the calla lilies for a dramatic effect.

MINI BAG BASKET
Small Flowers, Grass, Micro Flowers, Micro Butterflies.
Cut the top off of a yellow mini bag. Use the extra piece to fashion a handle and attach it with tape. Place the flower stickers, add two layers of grass, a few butterflies—then fill with Easter goodies.

EASTER GREETING CARD
Extravagant Rabbit, Small Flowers, Medium Easter Eggs, Chicks.
Use small flowers for the garland on the rabbit's head. Place the rabbit on the card, powdering the back of the ears. Cut a piece of green paper to make the grass, and attach it with mounting tape. Arrange the eggs and the chick in the grass.

Easter is a favorite theme at Mrs. Grossman's. These playful projects feature friendly critters and exquisite flowers that are bound to get things hopping at your house this Spring!

PEEK-A-BOO CARD
Micro Flowers, Easter Rabbit, Multi Bows, Grass.
Cut two pieces of paper (one yellow, one purple) into an egg shape. Cut a center window from the yellow piece. Attach both pieces at the top with tape, covering the area with a bow. Attach the bunny, basket and multiple layers of grass inside with mounting tape. Place the remaining micro flower stickers as shown and powder the inside edges.

BOUNDING BUNNIES GIFT BAG
Micro Flowers, Rabbit, Small Easter Eggs, Color Dots.
Arrange the stickers, wrapping the bunny as needed. Place two color dots at the top of the bag, punching holes through both. Lace ribbon through the holes, and decorate the ends with micro flowers.

EASTER EGGS GREETING CARD
Reflection Easter Eggs, Multi Bows.
Use metallic tape or a paint pen to create eye-catching egg strings.

STICKER BASKET
Medium Easter Eggs, Chicks.
Nest a roll of stickers (still on the liner paper) in a little straw basket to make a thoughtful (and useful) gift. Use the chicks back-to-back, and finish it off with a bow.

23

TIP: *Pointed tweezers are very useful when placing stickers.*

EASTER INVITATION
Reflection Easter Eggs, Small Flowers.
Create an invitation on your computer, or use a calligraphy pen and note card. Glue it to a larger piece of paper, and add a shiny border using metallic tape. Place the stickers on the invitation and envelope as shown.

PAPER BASKET AND GARDEN GIFT BAG
Grass, Lambs, Micro Flowers, Giant Garden, Cloud and Rain, Easter Rabbit, Giant Trees, Extravagant Geometrics.
Basket: Cut a bright paper cup in half. Use the extra piece to fashion a handle, attach it with tape and add the stickers.
Bag: Assemble the sticker designs on liner paper and place them as shown. The tops of the oak trees are used as bushes to add height. Powder the back of the cloud where it extends over the edge.

BIG BUNNY BASKET
Extravagant Rabbit, Medium Easter Eggs, Mrs. Grossman's Easter Egg Decorating Kit, Micro Flowers, Grass.
Arrange the grass along the basket front and tape it in place. Decorate the eggs with stickers and nest them in the basket. Cut the rabbit's hand to hold an egg, and powder the back. Add colorful ribbons with back-to-back micro flowers on the ends.

DECORATED EGGS
Mrs. Grossman's Easter Egg Decorating Kit, Color Dots.
Dye the eggs the colors of your choice, then use the sticker kit to create eggs that will rival the Easter Bunny's!

Springtime stickers inspire endless creativity! Which is your favorite design?

SUMMER HOLIDAYS

MOM'S MINI GIFT BAG
Tulips, Ivy, Multi Bows.
Assemble the design on liner paper and apply it to the center of the bag. Use a permanent ink pen to write a personal message to Mom.

GRAD'S GIFT CARD
Extravagant Neighborhood Dogs, Graduation Hats, Confetti.

DAD'S GREETING CARD
Extravagant Alphabet, Puppies, Giant Presents, Extravagant Neighborhood Dogs, Dancing Bear.
Guaranteed to please the top dog in your family!

FOURTH OF JULY INVITATION
Flag, Sparkle Stars.
Create the invitation on your computer and print it on white paper. Glue it to a larger piece of red paper, and apply those stickers!

PARTY POPPER
Flag, Sparkle Stars.
Pack party favors inside small cardboard tubes and wrap them with colorful paper. Twist and cut the paper ends into strips, and wrap them with floral wire. Apply stars back-to-back on the ends of the w

26

We've included some red-hot projects for all of your summer celebrations. There's Mother's Day, Father's Day, Graduation, the Fourth of July—but wait! Stickers are also great "helpers" when it comes to entertaining kids while traveling, or catching up on long overdue correspondence.

BARBECUE INVITATION
Insects, Giant Picnic, Giant Trees, Fast Food, Grass.
Cut a fence out of white paper that will fit on the blue card. Place the tree on the card, then attach the fence with glue or double-stick tape. Arrange the picnic scene, using mounting tape to bring some stickers forward. Trim an ice cream cone to make the chef's hat.

MONEY BOX
Extravagant Animal Expressions, Graduation Hats, Money.
Giving a check to that graduate? Wrap it up in a small box decorated with money stickers. Press two Pippa stickers, graduation hat and diploma back-to-back, leaving the toes unconnected. Attach Pippa to the box by her toes.

3-D BOUQUET CARD
Tulips, Iris, Freesia, Ivy.
Arrange the flowers on a piece of liner paper, then wrap a thin piece of rice paper around them. Powder the back of the stickers where they extend over the edge. Tie a gold ribbon around the paper and glue the bouquet to a green card.

KEY CHAIN
Small Alphabet, Baseball.
An adorable daily reminder for dad! Use a copy of a favorite photo and cut it to fit in a picture key chain. Cut the bat and arrange it on the photo with the remaining stickers.

27

TIP: *Use a light touch when placing stickers. You may decide to move them, or tuck another sticker underneath.*

GRADUATION INVITATION
Graduation Hats, Micro Stars.
Cut red and black paper to make a framed card. Print an invitation on your computer and cut it to fit on top as shown. Glue the papers together and add the stickers to the invitation and envelope.

FRUIT KABOBS
Fruit, Strawberries.
Place the stickers back-to-back on the ends of wooden toothpicks or skewers for a festive fruit plate.

FOURTH OF JULY CARD
Giant Trees, Giant Garden, Giant Fishing, Giant Musical Instruments, Giant House, Small Flags, Puppies, Dancing Bear, Chipmunks, Wagon, Bunnies, Penguins, Elephant, Micro Stars.
Arrange the trees, house, bear and fence on a piece of liner paper, then place them on a blue card. Attach the parade animals with mounting tape. Cut the elephant's hat from a flag. Glue a piece of matching paper to the envelope flap for a coordinated look.

KID CERTIFICATES
Blue certificate: Small Alphabet, Toys, Cars, Giant Bathtub, Giant Horse Tack, Giant Playground.
Pink certificate: Small Alphabet, Breakfast, Micro Flowers, Giant Musical Instruments, Extravagant Animal Expressions.
Yellow certificate: Small Alphabet, Grass, It's A Girl, Clothesline, Frog.
Cut out rectangular pieces of brightly colored paper and use alphabet stickers to write personal "good for" messages. The pink certificate uses a cut trumpet sticker to make a vase. The tray is made of colored paper, with silver paint pen highlights. Powder the hippo's legs where they extend beyond the edge.

When school's out—stickers are in!

HALLOWEEN

HALLOWEEN INVITATION
Extravagant Boo, Giant Trick-or-Treaters, Extravagant Geometrics.
Arrange the spooky scene on a purple card using mounting tape behind the ghosts, then write the greeting with a paint pen.

SKELETON GOODY BAG
Giant Skeleton, Small Jack-o'-lantern.
For a scary effect, cut a jagged edge along the top of a black mini bag. Apply the stickers as shown and fill it with yummy treats!

BOO-TIFUL GIFT BAG
Extravagant Boo, Jack-o'-lantern, Extravagant Neighborhood Dogs, Small Jack-o'-lantern, Halloween Candy, Giant Presents, Giant Pumpkin Faces, Party Hats, Buttons, Giant Beach.
Draw a picket fence on a white gift bag and carefully cut it out with an X-ACTO knife. Trim a green gift bag and nest it inside the white fence bag, then nest a purple gift bag inside the green one. Decorate with the stickers as shown, attaching the dogs, house and forward tree with mounting tape.

A chill in the air, pumpkins on the porch, and children dressed up for a night of spook-tacular fun. We hope these sticker projects help the days of waiting for Halloween fly by as quick as a friendly ghost!

GUESS WHO? GIFT CARD
Bears, Giant Pumpkin Faces, Giant Trick-or-Treaters, Top Hat.
Dress the bears while they're still on the liner paper, then place them on the card. Powder the areas where stickers extend over the edge.

STICKER GOODY BAG
Pumpkin, Scary Cat, Halloween Candy, Bats.
Cut the pumpkin across the middle in a jagged pattern. Create the sticker design on liner paper, then place it on the bag. Powder the cat where it extends over the edge. Fill the bag with treats—or better yet, stickers!

BEARY SCARY CARD
Bear, Giant Pumpkin Faces, Small Leaves.
Cut the tree and ground from black paper and glue them to a green card. Cut the tops off of the pumpkins and place them on the bears. Add the leaves, powdering the stickers where they extend over the edge.

WRAPPED CANDY APPLE
Extravagant Boo!, Micro Stars, Micro Sparkle Stars.
Cover candy apples with cellophane, then wrap them in orange tissue paper. Tie each one with purple ribbon, and decorate with stickers as shown. Place ghosts back to back.

31

 **TIP:** *Always cut stickers while they're still on the liner paper.*

HAUNTED PARTY INVITATION
Extravagant Boo!, Giant Skeletons, Small Alphabet, Small Jack-o'-Lantern, Small Ghosts.
Fold a 10" x 7" piece of black paper in half. Cut the top and right side in the shape of a haunted house. Cut the windows and door as shown, folding the door back. Draw spider and spider web inside windows. Cut a 10" x 7" piece of yellow paper in half. Hold it behind the black card and cut the roof line 1/8" larger. Glue the yellow card behind the front of the black card and add stickers as shown. (Note larger ghost is stuck on the inside of the black card.) You can print the invitation details on the remaining yellow card, cut to fit and glue to the inside of the black card.

LION MASK
Small Wild Animals, Jungle Leaves, Opalescent Multi Circles, Gold Stars, Opalescent Sun, Moon and Stars.
Make the mask and crown out of colored paper. Sticker the crown on liner paper and place on the lion's head. Finish with jungle leaves. Punch holes below the ears and use ribbon to tie the mask on.

PUMPKIN CUPCAKE
Giant Pumpkin Faces, Bats.
Glue googly eyes onto two jack-o'-lantern stickers, and place them back-to-back on a plastic skewer. Use the black bats to make a simply screeching coaster.

TRICK-OR-TREAT BAG AND MASK
Giant Pumpkin Faces, Opalescent Sun, Moon and Stars, Charms, Sparkle Small Stars.
Gather a couple of feathers and some purple satin ribbon, then simply apply these stickers to transform a plain mask and gift bag into extra fancy Halloween accessories!

Too much candy? Stickers make a terrific trick-or-treat alternative!

THANKSGIVING

PRETTY PLACE CARDS
Autumn Wreath, Christmas Bows, Turkey, Basket, Small Leaves, Vegetables, Autumn Border.
Use store-bought place cards or folded colored paper. For the wreath card, cut a semi-circle in center of folded card and place wreaths back-to-back. For basket card, cut the bottom off the basket, cut left handle at edge of basket, hold back and place vegetables, turkey and leaves as shown. Return handle to original position (behind vegetables). Third card is simply Autumn Border sticker. Option: use mounting tape for added dimension, and powder edges that extend beyond edge of card.

PILGRIM GIFT CARD
Pilgrims, Autumn Border.
Cut the autumn border to fit in front of the pilgrims.

HARVEST PHOTO FRAME
Small Leaves.
Cut a window from a green card and use colored paper to make contrasting mats around the inner edges. Tape a copy of a favorite photo inside the window, and decorate the frame with stickers. Glue a golden bow in the corner for added sparkle, then use a paint pen to write the date.

POP-UP GREETING CARD
Small Leaves, Turkey, Autumn Border, Christmas Bows.
Glue a piece of white specialty paper to a maroon greeting card, or piece of colored paper. Assemble the wreath on a piece of liner paper, layering the leaves and corn first, then adding the turkey and multiple bows for a dimensional look. Attach the wreath to the card with mounting tape.

THANKSGIVING CENTERPIECE
Giant Bear, Small Leaves, Turkey, Autumn Wreath, Small Apples, Pumpkins, Vegetables, Basket, Ivy.
Measure and cut a strip of colored paper to fit around a small pumpkin. Arrange the sticker design on liner paper, then place it on the paper. Powder the backs of the stickers where they extend over the edge. Wrap the band around the pumpkin and fasten with tape.

Changing colors, feeling thankful, scrumptious smells—and one funny looking bird! These sticker projects were created to encourage sharing, caring and enchanting entertaining experiences throughout the season of giving.

DELICIOUS MENU
Pilgrims, Small Leaves.
Write up your menu and print it out on a computer. Mount the menu on a larger piece of contrasting paper and decorate it with stickers. Finish it off with a metallic tape border, and slide it into a plastic frame.

TEXTURED GIFT CARD
Basket, Fruit, Small Leaves.
Cut a small piece of corrugated paper and glue it to a green gift card. Cut the left handle of basket, hold back and place fruit and leaves as shown. Return handle to original position (behind fruit). Attach basket to card with mounting tape.

KEEPSAKE RECIPE CARDS
Pumpkin, Small Leaves, Vegetables, Reflection Small Hearts, Turkey, Fruit.
Cut the top off the pumpkin and arrange the design on a piece of liner paper. Cut a Reflection Small Heart to create the spoon. Apply either design as shown to a recipe card.

ACCORDION ANIMAL CARD
Giant Woodland Animals, Giant Trees, Extravagant Geometrics, Halloween Candy.
Carefully tear three pieces of contrasting, natural-colored paper on a diagonal to make the mountains. The height of each piece should vary, as pictured. The back panel is a solid-colored sheet of paper. Tape the pieces together accordion-style. Apply the stickers, powdering the backs of any that extend beyond the edge. Use mounting tape to add even more depth. Glue small lengths of raffia along the front to create a meadow.

35

 **TIP:** *When cutting stickers, save the extra pieces for future art projects.*

CRANBERRY RELISH LABEL AND RECIPE CARD
Small Leaves, Fruit, Turkey, Autumn Border.
Use a plain label, or a small piece of white paper, and attach it to the jar with a border of over-the-edge stickers. Decorate a matching recipe card to top off this thoughtful homemade gift.

NAPKIN RINGS
Turkey, Autumn Border, Small Leaves, Christmas Bows, Pumpkin, Fruit, Halloween Candy.
Cut colored paper into strips. Create the sticker designs and attach them with mounting tape, powdering the back of the stickers (but not the tape) before applying them to the paper. Wrap the decorated strips around cloth napkins and tape the ends together in the back. To create added dimension, layer identical stickers on top of each other, bending up and powdering the sides of the top sticker.

THANKSGIVING GIFT BAG
Pilgrims, Small Leaves.
Cut out a circle of orange paper, decorate it with small leaves on the bottom edge and tape it to the bag. Punch two holes in the top of the bag and string a ribbon through so that both ends dangle in front. Make the design and attach it with mounting tape, powdering the back of the stickers (but not the tape) before applying it to the bag. Place small leaves on the ribbons back to back.

AUTUMN TRELLIS GREETING CARD
Autumn Wreath, Small Leaves.
Attach a wide piece of ribbon on the card using glue or double-stick tape. Cut the wreath stickers in half and arrange them on the ribbon as shown, tucking the edges under the ribbon as needed. Fill in the design with small leaves, and highlight with silver paint pen dots.

Autumn greetings to warm the heart.

CHRISTMAS

HUNGRY BAKER'S HOLIDAY CARD
Gingerbread Boys, Basket, Cooks, Extravagant Animal Expressions.
Trim a red card and attach it to a green card with mounting tape. Create the sticker design on a piece of liner paper, then center it on the red card. Pierre the alligator is wearing two chef hats; the one on top is attached with mounting tape. The batter is made from a cut up gingerbread boy.

SILENT NIGHT GIFT BAG
Opalescent Sun, Moon and Stars, Garland, Extravagant Trim-A-Tree, Giant Woodland Animals, Santa Hats.
Trim a white gift bag to look like rolling hills of snow. Cut tree silhouettes out of a green bag and nest it inside the white one. Cut scallops from the top of a blue bag and nest it inside of the green one. Add the stickers as shown, and use a permanent ink pen to make the tracks. Powder the animal stickers where they extend beyond the various edges.

SNOW FUN GREETING CARD
Snowman, Snow Tree, Skiing.
Trim a white card or paper into the shape of a snow bank and glue it to a blue card. Cut a snow tree down the middle, trim a bit off the bottom, and place it as shown. Arrange the skiing snowmen on a piece of liner paper, then place them on the slopes. Add those snowballs!

What's the perfect recipe for a wonderful winter holiday? Just mix family and friends, blend in some good food, sprinkle with a handful of excited children, and add lots of colorful stickers! Both Christmas and Chanukah provide endless opportunities to decorate cards, spruce up gifts and create homemade crafts like these:

ELEGANT PHOTO FRAME
Holly, Poinsettia.
Choose a copy of a prized photo and make a frame for it using sturdy red paper. Glue gold ribbon around the inner frame edge. Attach the frame to a white card and apply the stickers as shown.

WINTER TREE BOOKMARK
Reflection Winter Tree, Sparkle Small Snowflakes.
Cut a piece of satin ribbon to the desired length and attach matching stickers using the back-to-back method.

NUTCRACKER GIFT CARD
Nutcracker, Micro Hearts, Christmas Bows.
Arrange the design as shown, powdering the back of the bow where it extends over the edge.

OUR TOWN CHRISTMAS CARD
Townfolk, Christmas Rush, Christmas Houses.
Trim a white card or paper into the shape of a snowy street and glue it to a black card. Arrange the town scene stickers as shown, adding paint pen dots to create the falling snow.

39

A card filled with stickers sent before the holidays makes a welcome—and useful—gift!

CHANUKAH CARD
Sparkle Chanukah Accessories, Extravagant Christmas Hearth, Expressions Bear, Giant Presents, Small Presents.
Place the hearth, then arrange the other stickers as shown—or create your own cozy scene!

JINGLE BELLS CARD
Jingle Bells, Holly, Design Lines Primaries.
Trim a white card and attach it with mounting tape to a red card. Cut the Design Lines to the desired length and apply them to the card. Assemble the bells and holly on liner paper, then place them as shown.

CHANUKAH GARLAND BOOKMARK
Sparkle Chanukah Accessories.
Trim a sturdy piece of white paper to fit on a slightly larger blue piece. Draw a curvy line with a paint pen and decorate it with the stickers for a garland effect.

GINGERBREAD HOUSE GIFT BOX
Gingerbread House, Candy, Extravagant Trim-A-Tree.
Assemble the candy and house design on liner paper, then apply it to a green gift box. Scatter the remaining stickers around to fill out the design. Top it off with a great big bow.

40

Clean sticky scissors with a little rubbing alcohol.

STYLISH PLACE CARDS
Reflection Pine Cone, Reflection Ornaments, Silver and Gold Confetti.
Apply the designs to folded colored paper, powdering any areas that extend beyond the edge.

FUN WITH PHOTOS
Christmas Bows, Poinsettias, Design Lines Primaries.
A few stickers can showcase photos—without stealing the show! Use the Design Lines as borders to emphasize your theme.

BARK! THE HERALDS GREETING CARD
Extravagant Trim-A-Tree, Santa Hats, Christmas Garland, Extravagant Neighborhood Dogs.
Place the tree on a red card and decorate it with the ornaments. While still on the liner paper, dress up the dogs with the garland and bows. Place them as shown, using mounting tape to bring a few pups forward.

41

TIP: *Like a painting or sculpture, make sure to sign your original sticker art!*

DELUXE PRESENT AND 3-D TREE
Small Presents, Sparkle Toys, Extravagant Christmas Hearth, Santa, Toys, Extravagant Trim-A-Tree.
Present: Wrap a small present in white and red paper as shown. Apply the background stickers first, then work forward to create this jolly scene. Use mounting tape on some stickers for added depth.
Tree: Crease four matching trees down the middle while still on the liner paper. Match and attach two trees up to the crease marks only. Add another tree to the exposed half of one of the first two. Add the fourth tree to the remaining two exposed surfaces. Decorate the 3-D tree with ornaments. Cut a circle of red paper with craft scissors for the base. Anchor the tree by placing presents on each corner, folding the lower halves. Press onto base. For the stand-up presents, use the back-to-back method, leaving the bottom edges unconnected so you can attach them to the base around the tree.

PEEK-A-BOO COOKIE BAGS
Holly, Sparkle Bow, Extravagant Trim-A-Tree, Small Presents, Micro Stars.
Cut a fun shape out of the front of a colorful gift bag. Decorate the bag with stickers as shown, then fill a clear plastic bag with homemade treats and set it inside. Punch two holes in the top of the gift bag for a ribbon, or fold the top back and add a sticker bow, powdering the back where it extends over the edge.

CHRISTMAS STATIONERY
Candy, Gingerbread Men, Candy Canes, Sparkle Christmas Tree, Holly.
Start with plain note cards and add stickers to create your own Christmas stationery!

TIE-ON GIFT TAGS
Reflections Winter Tree, Jingle Bells, Sparkle Christmas Tree, Extravagant Trim-A-Tree.
Cut some squares of white paper, then attach them with mounting tape to larger squares of colored paper that have been cut with craft scissors. Arrange the stickers on each card, punch a hole at the top and add a contrasting ribbon. Tie a ribbon bow at the top of the bell for added fun.

From sentimental to silly, sticker designs spread holiday cheer.

RESOURCES

Congratulations—you're an official sticker artist! You've learned basic techniques and design skills, made dozens of creative crafts and (hopefully) had a great time in the process. Want to know more? We recommend these resources for additional sticker art information and inspiration:

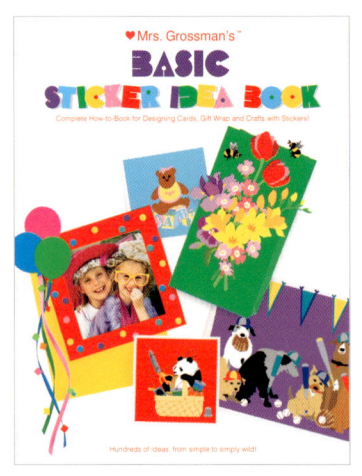

Basic Sticker Idea Book

Sticker Express Newsletter

STICKER LINER PAPER
Start by checking the back of Mrs. Grossman's liner paper for fresh sticker design ideas.

BASIC STICKER IDEA BOOK
Our first book is filled with exciting project themes including: Birthdays, Baby, At Home, School and Sports, Flowers and Photo Albums. An excellent companion for the Holiday Sticker Idea Book.

MRS. GROSSMAN'S VIDEOS
Watch the pros and learn their secrets! These dynamic, interactive videos demonstrate sticker art through friendly, hands-on projects.
- Sticker Magic
- Sticker Magic 2: *Creative Card Making*

STICKER EXPRESS NEWSLETTER
Let us deliver the latest sticker news to your home! Interested in a 6-issue yearly subscription? Call **800-429-4549** for more information.

MRS. GROSSMAN'S HOTLINE
Have questions? Can't find the right stickers? Stuck on a sticker project? Call **800-429-4549** for on-the-spot answers and advice.

VISIT OUR WEBSITE
A great resource for innovative stickering ideas and the latest news. Our address is: www.mrsgrossmans.com

Throughout this book, we have used Mrs. Grossman's cards, gift cards, bookmarks and bags. We have also used complementary products manufactured and distributed by the following companies:
- Crane Paper Company
- The Paper Company
- Webway Album Pages

MEET THE ARTISTS

How does anyone make such beautiful stickers? You only need to have the best artists who work together as one talent, who love to design happy, uplifting and sometimes downright silly images and won't stop until the work is done and done *right*. It's simple!

Take, for instance, **Gigi Sproul**, top row right. She has worked at MGPC for more than sixteen years and delights us with her marvelous humor. No assignment is too difficult; she relishes a challenge and has in fact, mastered all of the many facets of the art department.

Or **Melissa Carlson**, top row center, a creative dynamo in a gentle and sweet package. With MGPC for fourteen years, Melissa is our flower expert. But that's not all she does: she is equally proficient with package design and innovative product concepts.

Or **Susan Pratt**, top row left. A relative newcomer (only five years), Susan brings a graceful addition to the mix. Her years as a designer of children's clothing shows in her light-at-heart designs, but like Melissa, she loves variety and leaps at the opportunity to design new product.

Now **Julie Cohen**, bottom row left, has been with MGPC for fifteen years and is lovingly called "the Eye"- nothing gets by her. Even with an incredible eye for detail, she manages to get terrific energy and affection in her sticker designs.

Andrea Grossman, bottom row center, designed most of the original stickers (starting with the red heart in 1979) and now occasionally gets to design a new one. Her primary job as art director is to love these people- and *that* is a piece of cake.

Susanna Gallisdorfer, coming in from left field (where she spends a lot of her time), has designed stickers for years, many on staff, now by phone, mail and fax. Her stickers add a special whimsy to the line.

Now that you are acquainted, remember to look for the designers' names on the back of our stickers!

While they aren't pictured above, special credit goes to our terrific staff of support people: **Blythe Omick** and **Raul Chacon** take the designers' drawings from original to printable. **Linda Hendrickson** and **Audrey Giorgi** design original sticker art as well as numerous other creative assignments to produce what you see in this book.

STICKER CHECKLIST

Red Heart **R**	Micro Red&Pink Heart **R**	Small Red Heart **R**	Micro Hearts **R**	Cinnamon Hearts **R**	Confetti Heart **R**	Spectrum Heart **R**	Small Roses **R**	Rose **DR**	Pansy **R**	Sunflower **DR**	Pink Phlox **DR**	Freesia **DR**	
Tulip **DR**	Iris **DR**	Small Flowers **R**	African Daisy **R**	Micro Flowers **R**	Ivy **R**	Daffodils **R**	Calla Lily **R**	Garden Border **DR**	Pumpkin **R**	Small Leaves **R**	Autumn Wreath **R**	Autumn Border **R**	
Cloud and Rain **R**	Micro Stars **R**	Rainbow **R**	Gold Stars **R**	Jungle Leaves **DR**	Palm Tree **R**	Snow Tree **DR**	Grass **DR**	Fruit **DR**	Vegetables **DR**	Strawberries **R**	Small Apple **R**	Watermelon **R**	
Small Bears **R**	Bear **R**	Micro Butterflies **R**	Insects **DR**	Chipmunks **R**	Puppies **R**	Elephant **R**	Monkeys **DR**	Small Giraffe **DR**	Panda **R**	Small Wild Animals **DR**	Penguin **R**	Frogs **R**	
Kittens **R**	Lambs **R**	Bunnies **R**	Rabbit **R**	Dressed Mice **DR**	Expressions Bear **DR**	Expressions Cat **DR**	Expressions Dog **DR**	Dancing Bear **R**	Top Hat **R**	Silver and Gold Confetti **R**	Basket **R**	Blurb **R**	
Money **R**	Buttons **R**	Sweet Hearts **R**	Gardeners **R**	Cooks **R**	Doctors and Nurses **R**	Computer **R**	Telephone **R**	Graduation Hats **R**	Classroom Stuff **DR**	School **DR**	Small Flags **R**	Flag **R**	
Clothesline **DDR**	Travel Gear **DR**	Baseball **R**	Football Gear **R**	Golf **R**	Skiing **R**	Snow Toys **DR**	Skates **R**	Toys **DR**	Charms **R**	Tools **R**	Sewing **R**	Small Alphabet **DDR**	
	It's a Girl **R**	Color Dots **R**	Fast Food **R**	Dessert **R**	Breakfast **R**	Wagon **R**	Car **R**						

46

All the stickers we used in this book are shown here. This handy checklist makes it easy to find the stickers you need.

	Micro Multi Music Notes
	Pinwheels R
	Party R
	Balloon
	Birthday Cake R
	Party Hats DR
	Small Presents R
	Small Balloons R
	Confetti DR
	Candy R
	Bows, multi DR
	Chicks R
	Easter Basket R
	Easter Eggs, medium R
	Easter Eggs, small R
	Easter Rabbit DR
	Bats R
	Ghosts, small R
	Halloween Candy R
	Jack-o-Lantern R
	Jack-o-Lantern, small R
	Scary Cat R
	Pilgrims R
	Turkey R
	Candy Canes R
	Christmas Border DR
	Christmas Bows
	Christmas Candle R
	Garland R
	Gingerbread R
	Gingerbread House R
	Holly DR
	Holy Family R
	Jingle Bell R
	Stockings R
	Merry Christmas DR
	Christmas Houses
	Christmas Rush R
	Town Folk R
	Elves R
	Poinsettia R
	Reindeer DR
	Santa DR
	Santa, small R
	Santa Hats R
	Sleigh DR
	Snowman R
	Nutcrackers R
	Reflection Eggs RF
	Reflection Small Hearts DRF
	Reflection Watering Can RF
	Reflection Winter Tree RF
	Reflection Letters RF
	Reflection Ornaments RF
	Reflection Pine Cones RF
	Opal Multi Circles ●
	Opal Party Glasses ●
	Opal Sun, Moon, Sparkle Heart S
	Sparkle Small Red Hearts S
	Sparkle Multi Micro Hearts S
	Sparkle Small Hearts S
	Sparkle Toys S
	Sparkle Multi Micro Stars S
	Sparkle Micro Stars S
	Sparkle Bow S
	Sparkle Chanukah DS
	Sparkle Christmas Seal S
	Sparkle Christmas Tree S
	Sparkle Hugs & Kisses S
	Sparkle Jewel Hearts S
	Sparkle Small Stars S
	Sparkle Small Snowflakes S
	Giant Bathtub G
	Giant Bear G
	Giant Camping G
	Giant Cats G
	Giant Green Thumb G
	Giant Garden G
	Giant Horse Tack G
	Giant Red Heart G
	Giant Children G
	Giant Cottontails G
	Giant Fishing G
	Giant Skeletons G
	Giant Trick or Treaters G
	Giant Pumpkin Faces G

47

Giant Playground **G**
Giant Musical Instruments **G**
Giant Picnic **G**
Giant Presents **G**
Giant House **G**
Giant Trees **G**
Giant Woodland Animals **G**
Extravagant Alphabet **E**
Extravagant Geometrics **E**
Extravagant Vehicles **E**
Extravagant Animal Expressions **E**
Extravagant Neighborhood Dogs **E**
Extravagant Rabbit **E**
Easter Egg Decorating Kit
Design Lines Checkerboard Plus **DL**
Design Lines Primaries **DL**
Design Lines Basic Black and White **DL**
Extravagant Boo! **E**
Extravagant Trim-A-Tree **E**
Extravagant Christmas Hearth **E**

R	Regular	**S** Sparkle	**DRF** Double Reflection
DR	Double Regular	**DS** Double Sparkle	**G** Giant
DDR	Double Double Regular	**DDS** Double Double Sparkle	**E** Extravagant
●	Opalescent	**RF** Reflection	**DL** Design Lines

48